Guitar Method I
Book with Audio Access

by
Peter Vogl

For Acoustic or Electric Guitar

For Online Access to all of the audio files for this course, go to this web address:

http://cvls.com/extras/method/

INTRODUCTION

Guitar Method 1 is designed to help all guitarists learn to read traditional music notation. This includes beginners as well as accomplished guitarists that play by ear and would like to learn to read music. This clear step-by-step method represents the first major innovation in note reading books in the last 50 years and draws upon the extensive teaching experience of one of the world's leading guitar instructors. The method teaches you practical songs and scales that are currently used today which will enable you to apply what you have learned to the songs that you want to play. The Audio Tracks that come with this method are recorded by top studio musicians and will enable you to hear every exercise and example in this course. In addition, there are over 60 play along jam tracks that will let you play along with a full band, which not only is fun but will help you perfect your timing and ability to play with others. These tracks will also let you practice and perform for student recitals.

THE AUTHOR

Peter Vogl, the author of this book, has been a professional performer and teacher in the Atlanta area for over twenty years. He was raised in Michigan and went to college at the University of Georgia, where he majored in classical guitar performance. He also did post graduate work at James Madison University. Peter has set up and directed six different schools of music in the Atlanta area and currently works at Jan Smith Studios as a session player and guitar instructor. He has written several instructional courses including *I Blues Guitar Book & DVD, Rock Guitar Book & DVD, The Guitarist's Tablature Book, The Guitarist's Chord Book, The Guitarist's Scale Book, The Guitarist's Music Theory Book, Electric Licks & Solos, Country Licks & Solos,* and the *Let's Jam! CD Series* (nine different jam along CDs).

WATCH & LEARN PRODUCTS REALLY WORK

For over 25 years, Watch & Learn has revolutionized music instructional courses by developing well thought out, step by step instructional methods that were tested for effectiveness on beginners before publication. Each course is developed by top instructors that actively teach and are in touch with the current needs of students. Coupled with the consistent high standards of Watch & Learn, this has dramatically improved the success and enjoyment of beginning musicians and has set the standard for music instruction today. This easy to understand course will help you tremendously on your journey to having fun and becoming a well rounded guitarist.

AUDIO ACCESS

All of the audio tracks for this course are available online. Go to this web address:

http://cvls.com/extras/method/

THE AUDIO TRACKS

There are two sets of Audio Tracks with this book. *Set 1 - Exercises* contains all of the exercises in the book. The audio is mixed with the metronome on the right channel and the guitar on the left channel so you can isolate the metronome if you like. *Set 2 - Songs* contains all of the songs performed with a live band. There are two versions of each song, one with guitar playing along with the band and a second version with only the band so you can play along.

COMPANION PRODUCTS

The Guitarist's Chord Book by Peter Vogl is a 144 page book that contains over 900 chords with photos to clearly illustrate each chord and each note of the chord is labeled. This kindle edition makes finding chords you want to play easy. It also contains a special moveable chords section with the most widely used shapes for each class of chord. Peter Vogl has also included goodies from his bag of tricks to give you new sounds, shapes, and inspirations for song arrangements. The chord shapes have been reviewed by guitar teachers and players across the country. This is a must read for guitar players of all levels.
http://a.co/0p9B0C5

The Guitarist's Scale Book by Peter Vogl is a complete scale encyclopedia for guitar with over 400 scales and modes. It contains scale diagrams with notation and tablature for each scale and tips on how and when to use each scale.

This scale book also contains outside jazz scales, exotic scales, Peter's own Cross-Stringing scales, and easy to understand explanations of scales and modes. This is the only guitar scale book you'll ever need.
http://a.co/eX9tWMf

The Guitarist's Music Theory Book by Peter Vogl is the first music theory book designed for guitar by a guitarist. The book explains music theory as it applies to the guitar and covers intervals, scales, chords, chord progressions, and the Nashville Number System. You will also get online access to audio examples of all the music in the book and also an ear training section. The Music Theory Book was written to help all guitar players achieve a better understanding of the guitar and of the music they play.
http://a.co/3l4s9IZ

FOLLOW-UP PRODUCTS

Guitar Method 2 by Peter Vogl is the follow-up to *Guitar Method 1*. Learn chords & strumming, major scales, blues scales, pentatonic scales, playing up the neck, and arpeggios. The book comes with 2 audio CDs - one for exercises and one for performing. All 29 songs are recorded in two versions, with the guitar and without the guitar, giving the student a perfect piece for recital or performance.
http://a.co/bdnr7TK

TABLE OF CONTENTS

SECTION 4 - SHARPS, FLATS, AND KEY SIGNATURES

SECTION 5 - HARMONY AND CHORDS

SECTION 1
GETTING STARTED

For Online Access to all of the audio files for this course, go to this web address:

http://cvls.com/extras/method/

THE GUITAR

Your guitar should be stored in a neutral environment. This means not too cold, not too hot, not too wet, and not too dry. The wood in a guitar is subject to change and will expand or contract in response to its environment. Too much of any of these things could cause permanent damage. For example, never leave your guitar in your car for long periods of time during summer or winter months. Attics and basements tend to be poor locations for storing a guitar as well.

If you use a strap with your guitar to stand up and play, always keep a hand on the guitar. Straps won't always hold and a guitar falling from that height is never good. You can purchase strap locks to add another level of security, but if the strap itself breaks, the guitar may still fall.

The following photo shows the parts of a steel string guitar.

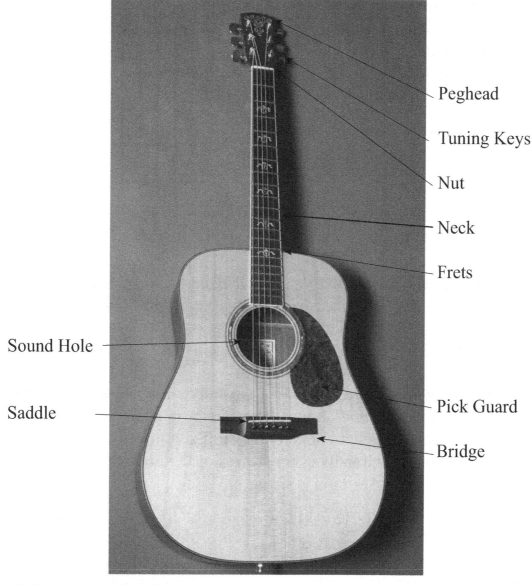

 TIP
Purchase a music stand. People who use one tend to practice up to 30% longer.

1

TUNING THE GUITAR

Before playing the guitar, it must be tuned to standard pitch. If you have a piano at home, it can be used as a tuning source. The following picture shows which note on the piano to tune each open string of the guitar to.

Note: If your piano hasn't been tuned recently, the guitar may not agree perfectly with a pitch pipe or tuning fork. Some older pianos are tuned a half step below standard pitch. In this case, use one of the following methods to tune.

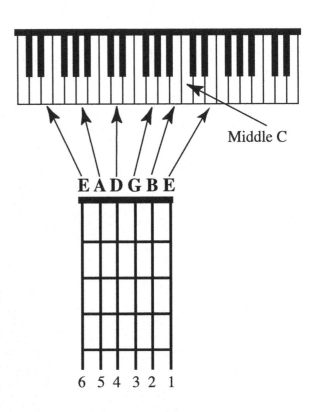

AUDIO TRACKS

It is recommended that you tune your guitar to the Audio Tracks that accompanies this book so that you will be in tune when you play along with the songs and exercises.

ELECTRONIC TUNER

An electronic tuner is the fastest and most accurate way to tune a guitar. I highly recommend getting one. It may take months or years for a beginner to develop the skills to tune a guitar correctly by ear. Even then the electronic tuner is more precise and used by virtually every professional guitar player.

TIP *Never leave your instrument in a car or trunk during extreme heat or cold.*

RELATIVE TUNING

Relative tuning means to tune the guitar to itself and is used in the following situations:

1. When you do not have an electronic tuner or other source to tune from.
2. When you have only one note to tune from.

In the following example we will tune all of the strings to the 6th string of the guitar, which is an E note.

1. Place the ring finger of the left hand behind the 5th fret of the 6th string to fret the 1st note. Tune the 5th string open (not fretted) until it sounds like the 6th string fretted at the 5th fret.
2. Fret the 5th string at the 5th fret. Tune the 4th string open (not fretted) until it sounds like the 5th string at the 5th fret.
3. Fret the 4th string at the 5th fret. Tune the 3rd string open until it sounds like the 4th string at the 5th fret.
4. Fret the 3rd string at the 4th fret. Tune the 2nd string until it sounds like the 3rd string at the 4th fret.
5. Fret the 2nd string at the 5th fret. Tune the 1st string open until it sounds like the 2nd string at the 5th fret.

Now repeat the above procedure to fine tune the guitar. Until your ear develops, have your teacher or a guitar playing friend check the tuning to make sure it is correct.

The following diagram of the guitar fret board illustrates the above procedure.

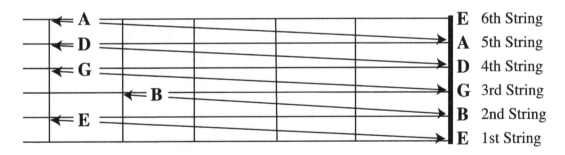

Note - Old dull strings lose their tonal qualities and sometimes tune incorrectly. Check with your teacher or favorite music store to make sure your strings are in good playing condition.

Always keep an extra set of strings in your case.
You never know when you will break one.

HOLDING THE GUITAR

CASUAL POSITION

There are two basic sitting positions for holding the guitar. The first and most common is the casual position. Sit erect with both feet on the floor and the guitar resting on your right thigh. The guitar should be braced against your chest with the right forearm so that the neck of the guitar doesn't move much when you change hand positions.

CLASSICAL POSITION

The second position is the classical position. Sit erect with your right foot on the floor and your left foot elevated on a footstool. The guitar rests on your left leg with the neck elevated. This position allows for a better back position and may make it easier for those who have back pain. It also allows for more freedom of movement of the left arm by raising the guitar neck and removing the left leg as an obstacle.

STANDING POSITION

When standing and using a strap, keep the guitar elevated for better technique, somewhere around waist high to chest high, depending on your build. Use a good strap or it may cause discomfort in the shoulders. A wide strap distributes the weight of the guitar better and is recommended.

TIP *Always use a case or gig bag when transporting your instrument from one place to another.*

THE PICK

SELECTING THE PICK

When you visit a music store, you will notice that there are almost as many pick styles and shapes as there are guitar players. A pick should feel comfortable in your hand and produce a clear, clean tone when picking or strumming the strings. This is the most popular pick shape.

HOLDING THE PICK

The grip on a pick should provide control while feeling comfortable. The most common way of holding the pick is to curl the right index finger (Figure 1), place the pick in the first joint of the index finger with the point facing straight out (Figure 2), and then place the thumb firmly on the pick with the thumb parallel to the first joint (Figure 3).

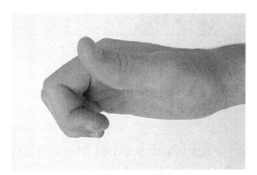

Figure 1

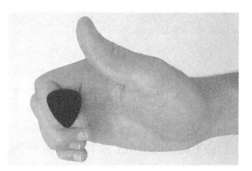

Figure 2

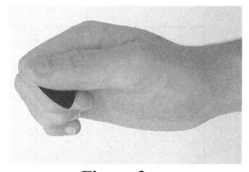

Figure 3

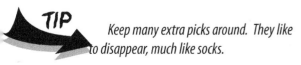

TIP *Keep many extra picks around. They like to disappear, much like socks.*

RIGHT HAND POSITION

Position the right hand so that the pick strikes the strings between the bridge and the fretboard. The top of the right forearm should be braced against the body of the guitar so that the right hand falls into a position towards the center of the sound hole. Do not rest your wrist or palm on the bridge. Too close to the bridge produces a bright tone and too far forward produces a tone that may be too dark. The right hand should be free with no part of the hand or wrist touching the guitar.

Bright   Correct   Too Dark   Wrist Not Resting on Guitar

LEFT HAND FINGERS

The index finger is the first finger, the middle finger is the second finger, the ring finger is the third finger and the pinky is the fourth finger. The thumb is not given a number since it is on the back of the neck.

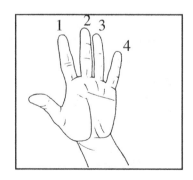

Use a guitar cloth to clean your guitar and wipe it down after you play.

LEFT HAND POSITION

When positioning your left hand on the guitar, pay careful attention to several things. The left elbow should hang freely to the outside of the left leg. Don't let your elbow creep into a position resting on the left leg or more into the body. This will avoid undue stress on the elbow and wrist. The hand itself should be positioned so the fingers can stay in front of the guitar neck.

THUMB POSITION

The thumb placement can vary a little due to hand and body size. Our basic thumb position will be around half way up the back of the guitar neck. This is our *core position*, meaning use this position most of the time. There will be times when we use an elevated thumb position, but this may compromise technique. We will discuss when to do this at a later time. Smaller hands should have an even lower thumb placement. This allows for better stretching and finger dexterity.

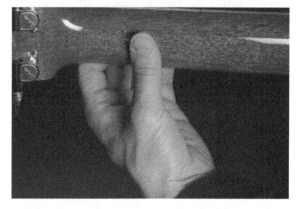

WRIST POSITION

The wrist should be below the guitar neck, which is our *wrist core position*.

TIP

A guitar should have a set-up every 6 months or so. Check with your local music store for this service.

WHAT FRETS MEAN TO YOU

Frets are the little metal bars on the neck of the guitar. When pressing down on a string in a fret space, the sound of the note comes from the fret in front of the finger (or to the left in the photo below). This is very, very important. What this means is **when we are pressing down any string in any fret, we are not trying to hold the string against the wood of the guitar neck**. (Read above phrase again as reinforcement). We are holding the string down so it touches the fret in front of it.

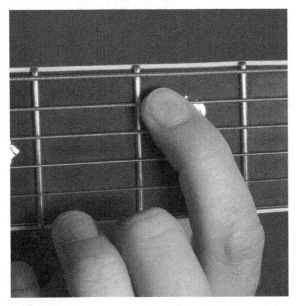

Finger at front of fret and good position

Finger in back of fret and poor position

CHORD DIAGRAMS

In this book you will find chord diagrams that will help you visualize where fingers should be placed on the guitar. Study the diagram below so that you will understand these diagrams when you see them.

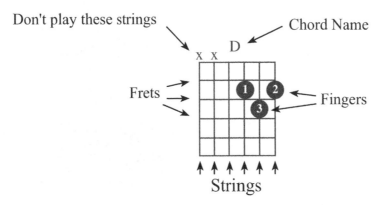

Once the frets on a guitar have large divots, they need to be replaced. This is called a fret job.

SECTION 2
THE STAFF, NOTES, AND
OPEN STRINGS

For Online Access to all of the audio files for this course, go to this web address:

http://cvls.com/extras/method/

NOTE PARTS

Notes can have several different parts depending on what type of note they are.

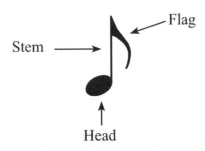

NOTE RHYTHMS

The type of note tells us how many beats to hold it or what rhythm to play. A whole note, which is a hollow note head, typically lasts for four beats or counts. The half note, which has a hollow head and a stem, lasts for two beats. The quarter note, which has a solid head and a stem, lasts for one beat. The eighth note has a solid head, a stem and one flag and lasts for half of a beat. (Two eighth notes last the same amount of time as one quarter note). The sixteenth note has a solid head, stem, and two flags. It lasts for a quarter of a beat (Four sixteenth notes lasts the same amount of time as a quarter note).

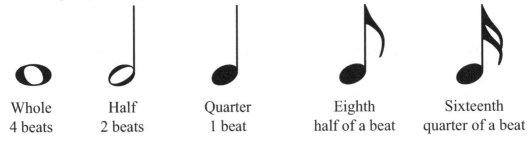

The diagram below shows how many half, quarter, eighth, and sixteenth notes it would take to last the same amount of time as a whole note. Two half notes equal one whole note. Two quarter notes equal one half note. Two eighth notes equal one quarter note. Two sixteenth notes equal one eighth note.

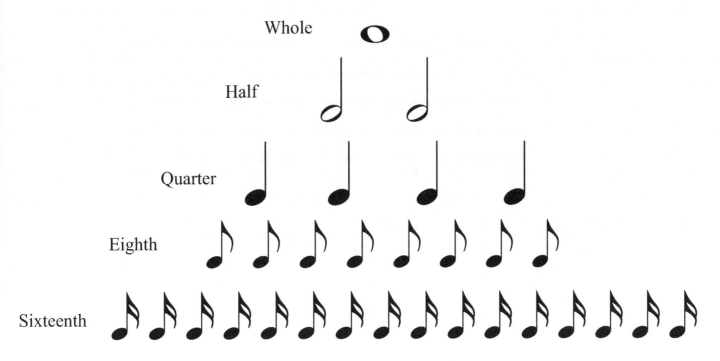

RESTS

When reading music, we also need to know when not to play. Rests tell us how much time to wait before we play again.

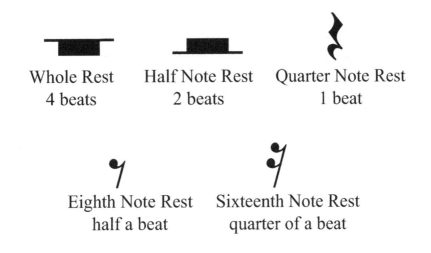

THE STAFF

The staff is where we place the notes telling us what pitch to play. The staff is made up of ledger lines and spaces.

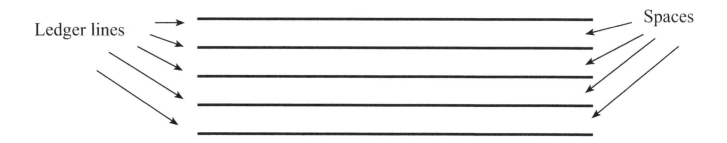

Ledger lines   Spaces

There are several elements added to the staff giving us more information. The clef sign tells us what pitches the lines and spaces represent. When playing guitar we use the treble clef.

Treble Clef

The treble clef sign tells us that the lines and spaces represent specific pitches. The spaces from the bottom up are the pitches F, A, C, E. The lines from the bottom up are E, G, B, D, F.

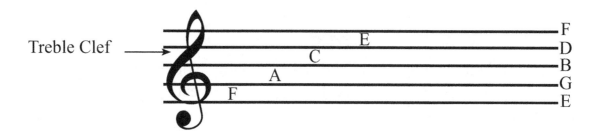

Treble Clef

Practice slow and relaxed.

12

BAR LINES

Bar lines are added to the staff to divide it into smaller units called measures or bars. This will make the staff easier to read and it will also tell us information about the rhythms and what notes are accented. Typically we accent the first beat in a measure. We will learn more about this as we learn about time signature.

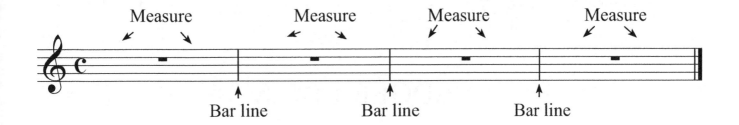

TIME SIGNATURE

Time signature is a symbol that tells us how many beats are in a measure. There are many time signatures and a few that are used more than others. Below are examples of the most frequently used time signatures.

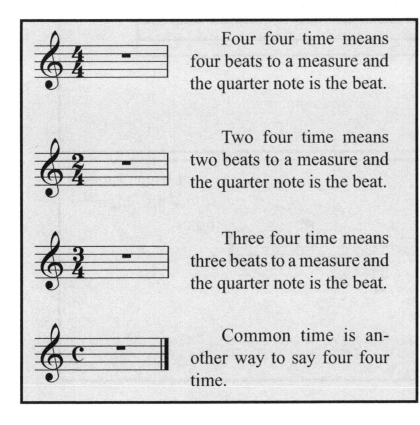

Four four time means four beats to a measure and the quarter note is the beat.

Two four time means two beats to a measure and the quarter note is the beat.

Three four time means three beats to a measure and the quarter note is the beat.

Common time is another way to say four four time.

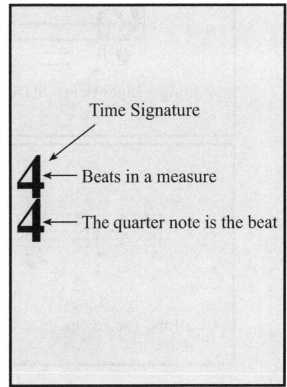

Time Signature

Beats in a measure

The quarter note is the beat

13

NOTES ON THE STAFF

Now we can see what the notes actually look like on the staff. Notes lower on the staff are lower in pitch. Notes higher on the staff are higher in pitch.

Lower Notes   Higher Notes

LEDGER LINES

We can go higher or lower than the five lines and spaces that make up the staff by adding extra ledger lines. It is like adding a line to the staff but we use just a small line. The reason we do this is to make the staff easier to read. Otherwise we would need a staff with many lines and spaces.

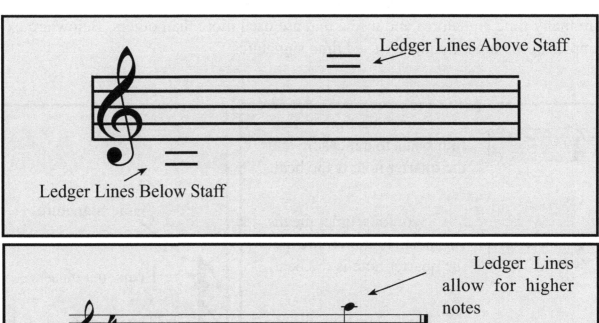

Ledger Lines Above Staff

Ledger Lines Below Staff

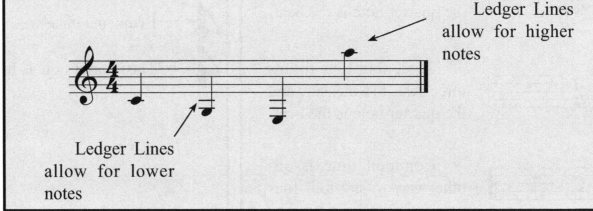

Ledger Lines allow for higher notes

Ledger Lines allow for lower notes

TIP *Heavier gauge strings offer more tone due to their thickness.*

14

OPEN 1ST, 2ND, AND 3RD STRINGS

CD1 2

Here are the notes representing the first three open strings on the guitar. It is important to memorize notes as we introduce them. Otherwise you will have difficulty playing the exercises or advancing your note reading skills.

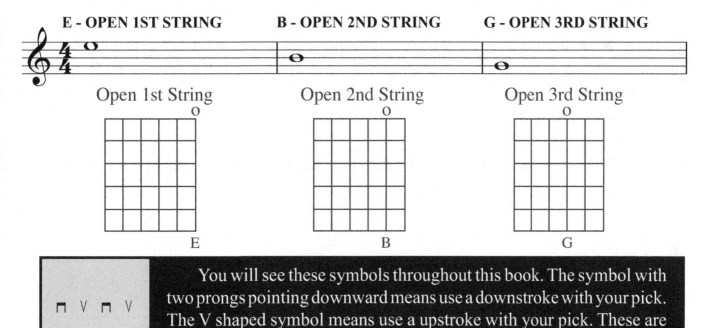

E - OPEN 1ST STRING   **B - OPEN 2ND STRING**   **G - OPEN 3RD STRING**

Open 1st String   Open 2nd String   Open 3rd String

E   B   G

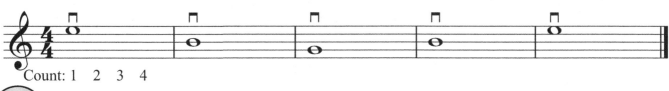

⊓ V ⊓ V   You will see these symbols throughout this book. The symbol with two prongs pointing downward means use a downstroke with your pick. The V shaped symbol means use a upstroke with your pick. These are suggestions that help you play more smoothly.

CD1 3

Exercise 1

This exercise will help you learn the first three open strings. Remember whole notes last for four beats. In all exercises the pick directions are only suggestions. If playing with fingers (right hand) try alternating the index and middle finger. The most important items to focus on are playing the correct notes and playing in time.

Count: 1 2 3 4

CD1 4

Exercise 2

This exercise demonstrates the open strings and playing half notes. Remember half notes last two beats.

Count: 1 2 3 4

15

Exercise 3

In this exercise we are primarily playing quarter notes. A quarter note lasts one beat. Alternate the pick directions. When you are given pick directions for only the first measure, it means you can generally repeat this pattern throughout the exercise or tune.

Count: 1 2 3 4

Exercise 4

This exercise will use a variety of rhythms. Practice playing the first three open strings and playing the correct rhythms.

Count: 1   2   3   4   1   2   3   4   1   2   3   4   1   2   3   4

1   2   3   4   1   2   3   4

OPENINGS

This tune highlights an Em arpeggio. *Arpeggio means to play one note of a chord at a time*. This song and many others in this book have a background track to play along with. One track is an example with melody and background music. Another track is just the background music allowing you to play the melody. There is a four beat click or count off before you are to begin playing. The chords used to accompany each tune are written above the staff.

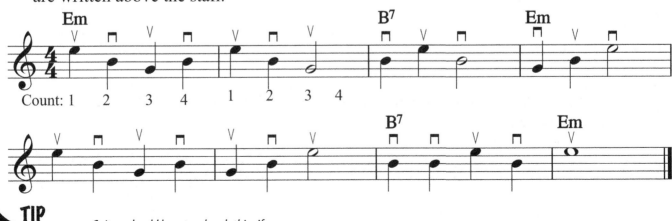

Count: 1   2   3   4   1   2   3   4

TIP *Guitars should be set up by a luthier if you change gauges of strings.*

16

OPEN 6TH, 5TH AND 4TH STRINGS

Here are the lowest three open strings on the guitar. Memorize them and move on to the next exercise.

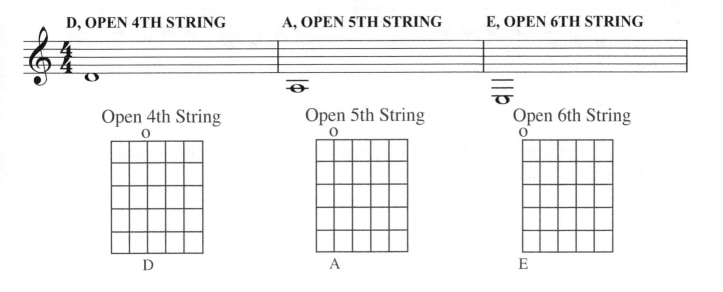

Exercise 5

This whole note exercise will help you learn the bottom three open strings on the guitar. Practice smoothly and evenly.

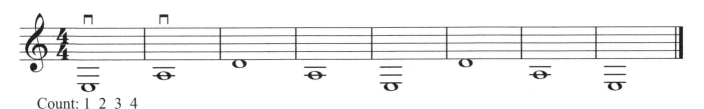

Count: 1 2 3 4

Exercise 6

Practice this half note exercise on the lowest three open strings.

Count: 1　2　3　4

TIP

Electronic tuners are the best way to tune a guitar.

Exercise 7

Practice this quarter note exercise on the bottom three open strings.

Count: 1   2   3   4

Exercise 8

This exercise incorporates a wider variety of rhythms. Remember to play in time and keep an even tempo.

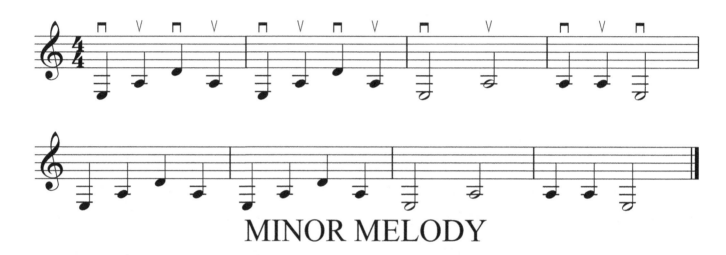

MINOR MELODY

Play the following with the band and use all six open strings. This tune will test how well you have learned to read all the open strings. When playing with the track, there is a four beat count off before you begin.

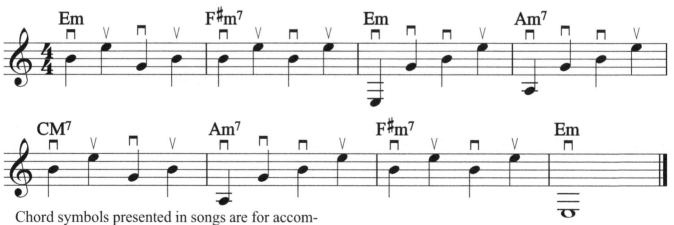

Chord symbols presented in songs are for accompaniment. These are also the chords used on the play along track.

18

SECTION 3
1ST POSITION NOTES

For Online Access to all of the audio files for this course, go to this web address:

http://cvls.com/extras/method/

NOTES ON THE 1ST STRING

Here are the notes going up the first string to the 5th fret. Memorize these notes. Notice that we are teaching the A note in this course which allows us to play a wider variety of melodies and use the little finger.

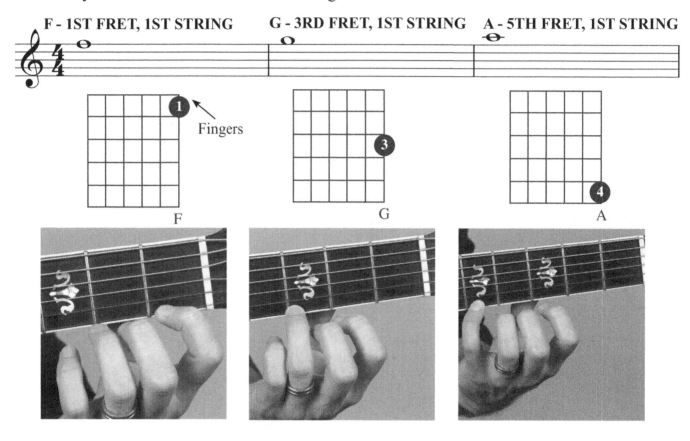

F - 1ST FRET, 1ST STRING **G - 3RD FRET, 1ST STRING** **A - 5TH FRET, 1ST STRING**

Fingers

F   G   A

Exercise 9

Practice this exercise playing whole notes on the 1st string.

Count: 1 2 3 4

Exercise 10

Practice this exercise playing half notes. Practice slow and relaxed. Notice the half note rest in the last measure.

Count: 1   2   3   4

Exercise 11

Practice this exercise playing quarter notes on the 1st string. Notice the whole note in the last measure.

Exercise 12

This exercise will get a little more interesting. Practice reading the notes and playing in time.

Exercise 13

Here is another exercise playing the notes on the 1st string. There are two audio tracks for this exercise. One is faster than the other to demonstrate playing these exercises at different speeds.

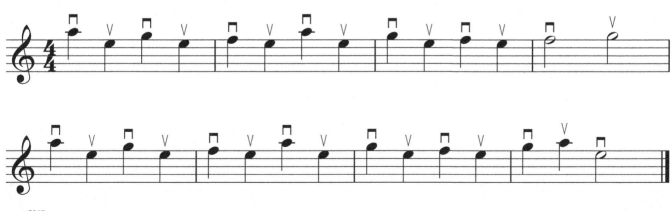

 Relaxation is a must for better technique.

21

NOTES ON THE 2ND STRING

Here are the notes we must learn on the 2nd string. Memorize them before moving on. The open second string is included even though we have already been introduced to it.

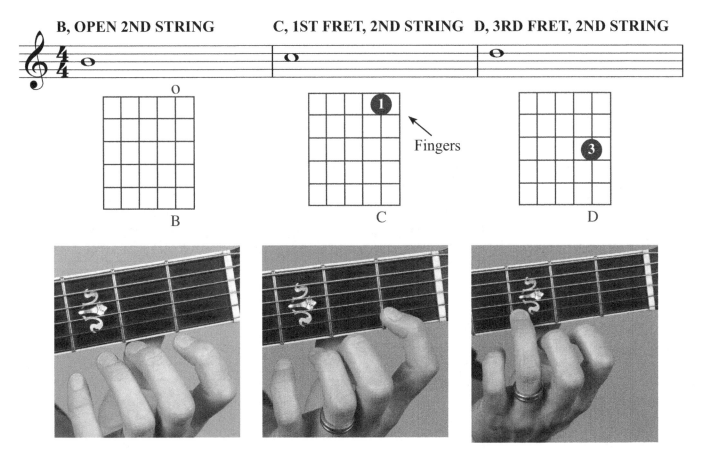

B, OPEN 2ND STRING **C, 1ST FRET, 2ND STRING** **D, 3RD FRET, 2ND STRING**

Fingers

B   C   D

Exercise 14

Practice this exercise playing whole notes on the 2nd string.

Count: 1 2 3 4

Exercise 15

Practice this exercise playing half notes. Play smooth and even.

Count: 1 2 3 4

Exercise 16

Practice this exercise playing quarter notes on the 2nd string.

Count: 1   2   3   4

Exercise 17

This exercise will use a variety of rhythms and notes on the 2nd string. Play in time and keep an even tempo.

Count: 1 2 3 4   1 2 3 4

Exercise 18

Here is another exercise using a variety of rhythms on the 2nd string.

ONTO BLUES

This melody has a blues flavor to it. Many of the songs in this book have a recorded track to play along with. First practice on your own and then play along with the band. Wait for the 4 beat count off to start.

Chord symbols presented in songs are for accompaniment. These are also the chords used on the play along track.

This is a repeat sign. It means go back to the beginning or previous repeat sign and start again.

BASICALLY A MINOR

This tune incorporates some of the open strings that we learned earlier. Wait for the four beat count off to play with the band.

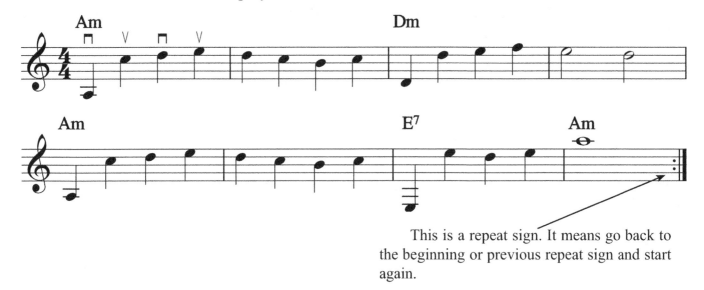

This is a repeat sign. It means go back to the beginning or previous repeat sign and start again.

THE PEDAL

This song highlights the use of pedal tones. *A pedal tone is a repeating note* and in this case, they are all low open strings. Practice until you can play this tune smoothly and then try playing along with the track. Wait for the four beat count off to begin.

TIP *There are no hands too big or too small for guitar if you use good technique.*

NOTES ON THE 3RD STRING

Here are the notes we will play on the 3rd string. Work on memorizing them as you play the next exercises.

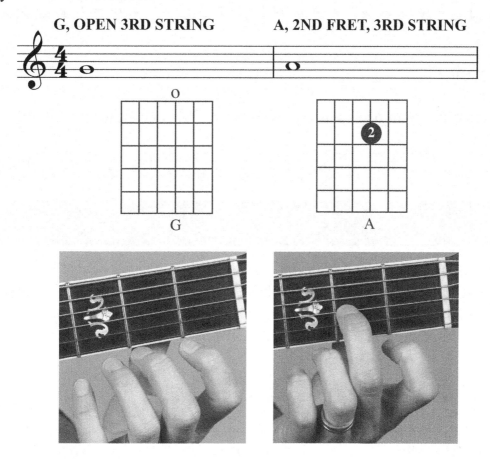

G, OPEN 3RD STRING   **A, 2ND FRET, 3RD STRING**

Exercise 19

Practice this exercise playing whole notes.

Count: 1 2 3 4

Exercise 20

Practice this exercise playing half notes.

Count: 1 2 3 4

25

Exercise 21

Practice this exercise primarily playing quarter notes.

Count: 1 2 3 4

Exercise 22

This exercise will use a variety of rhythms. Practice slow and smooth.

THE PICK UP

A pick up is a bar at the beginning of a tune that has fewer beats than usual. Many times this is balanced with an ending bar that is incomplete as well. Together they would make up a complete bar. Below are several examples. To count a pick up correctly, you should count the full bar and begin playing on the appropriate beat.

Exercise 23

This exercise has a two beat pick up to start.

Count: 3 4

26

CHORD TONES

This tune uses arpeggios (one note of a chord played at a time) and moves through the strings. Practice and then play with the band. Wait for the four beat count off.

AURA LEE

This tune is a well known melody. Make sure to count evenly as you play. Practice playing with the track and wait for the four beat count off to begin. Notice the repeat sign in the 4th measure.

 TIP *Use a metronome or drum machine to practice playing in time.*

27

8 BARS OF BLUES

This tune has an eight bar blues feel. Practice on your own and then try playing with the band. Wait for the 4 beat count off to start.

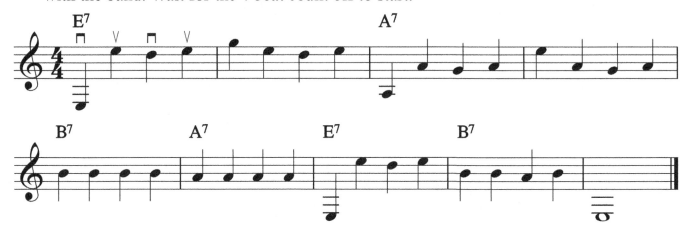

WHEN THE SAINTS GO MARCHING IN

Here is another song with a pick up at the beginning. There are only three beats in the first measure, so start playing on beat 2. Count 1 and, then begin on beat 2. When playing with the band, there is a four beat count off and then the first measure, which is a pick up, begins. The dotted half notes in line 3 are explained on page 43.

NOTES ON THE 4TH STRING

Here are the notes we will learn on the 4th string. Work on memorizing them as you play through the next exercises.

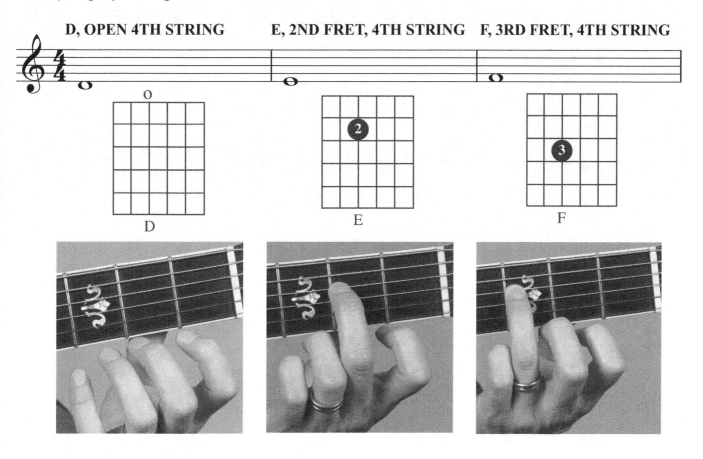

D, OPEN 4TH STRING **E, 2ND FRET, 4TH STRING** **F, 3RD FRET, 4TH STRING**

Exercise 24

Practice this exercise using whole notes.

Count: 1 2 3 4

Exercise 25

Practice this exercise using half notes.

Count: 1 2 3 4

Exercise 26

Practice this exercise primarily playing quarter notes.

Count: 1 2 3 4

Exercise 27

This exercise uses a variety of rhythms. Count slowly and evenly.

RING TONES

More arpeggios are in this next tune. Practice slowly and then try playing with the band after the four beat count off. The numbers under the staff are fingerings.

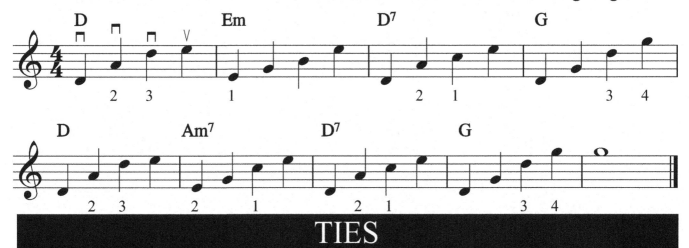

TIES

A tie connects two note values together. In example one, the tie connects a quarter note C to a half note C. We play only the first C and it now lasts for 3 beats. Simply add the quarter note to the half note and we get three beats. In example two, a half note C is added to another half note C across the bar line. Play only the first C and it should now last for a total of four beats (Two in the first measure and two in the second measure).

WILL THE CIRCLE BE UNBROKEN

This song starts with a two beat pick up. When playing with the track, there is a six beat count off to start. This includes the four beats before the first measure and the two beats at the front end of the pick up bar. The ties are explained on page 30.

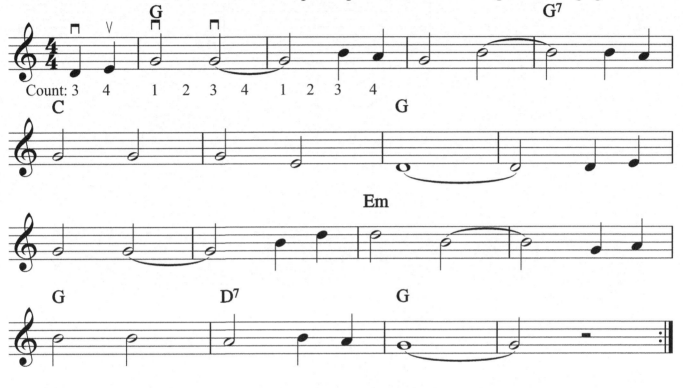

WALTZ IN G

This song is in 3/4 time. Count 1, 2, 3, 1, 2, 3. To get more exact with your timing, try counting 1 and 2 and 3 and. There is a 6 beat count off to begin.

31

NOTES ON THE 5TH STRING

Here are the notes we will learn on the 5th string. Work on memorizing them as you play the next few exercises.

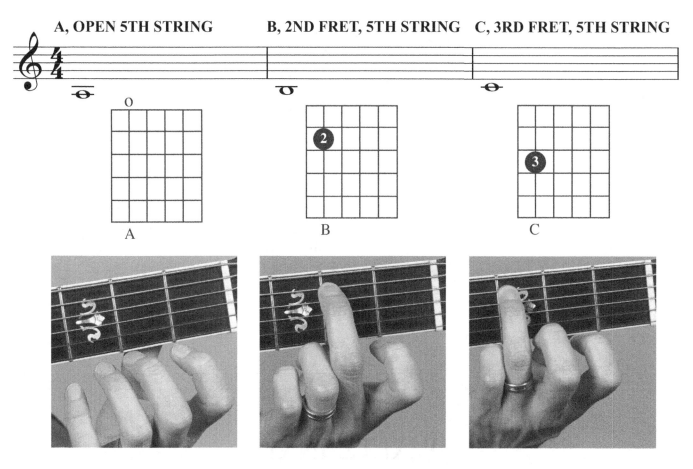

A, OPEN 5TH STRING   **B, 2ND FRET, 5TH STRING**   **C, 3RD FRET, 5TH STRING**

Exercise 28

Practice this exercise playing whole notes.

Count: 1 2 3 4

Exercise 29

Practice this exercise playing half notes.

Count: 1 2 3 4

Exercise 30

Practice this exercise primarily playing quarter notes.

Count: 1 2 3 4

Exercise 31

This exercise uses a variety of rhythms so make sure you are counting.

THE C MAJOR AND A MINOR SCALES

A scale is simply a series of single notes. There are many scales to choose from and they are used to create melodies and solos. They are also the basis for the key we are in. This is a concept to be discussed later. For now, here are two commonly used scales. Practice them both as they will prove extremely useful in your musical development. The numbers under the staff are fingerings. You will find many suggested fingerings throughout the rest of this book.

Exercise 32

This exercise is a C major scale. Practice until you can play it smoothly.

3   2   3   2   1   1   2   3   2   3

Exercise 33

This exercise is an A minor scale. This one goes two octaves. Practice it slowly and then work on speeding it up.

2   3   2   3   2   1   3   1   3   4

33

EIGHTH NOTES

We are now going to start using eighth notes in our exercises and songs. Remember, an eighth notes lasts for only half the time of a quarter (or half a beat). It is usually best to count eighth notes 1 and 2 and 3 and 4 and. When eighth notes are connected together, they are often done so by using a beam. This makes it easier to read a series of eighth notes. We must also learn to use eighth notes rests.

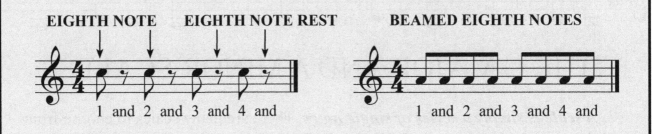

Exercise 34

Practice this exercise playing eighth notes. Be careful with the eighth note rests.

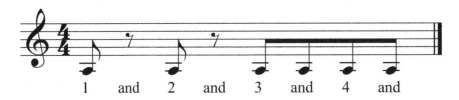

Exercise 35

Here is another exercise with eighth notes.

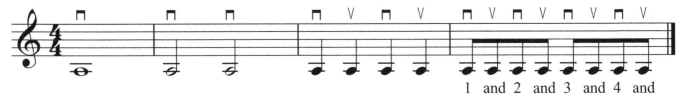

MAJOR SCALE MELODY

This song highlights the use of eighth notes and the C major scale. Practice slowly and evenly and then try playing with the band. Wait for the four beat count off to start.

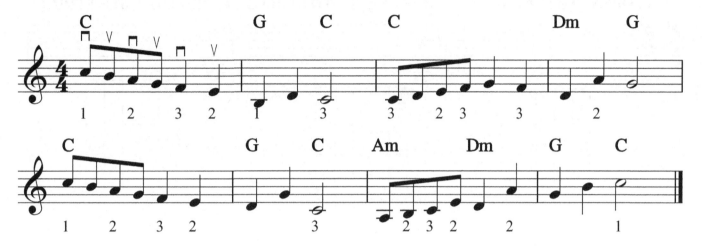

STRAIGHT EIGHT BLUES

This is a 12 bar blues form. Play the eighth notes evenly. When you are able, try playing with the track on the Audio Tracks. Wait for a four beat count off to start.

 **TIP** *Whenever transporting a guitar, be sure and use a guitar case or gig bag.*

35

NOTES ON THE 6TH STRING

Here are the notes we will learn on the 6th string. Work on memorizing them as you play the next few exercises.

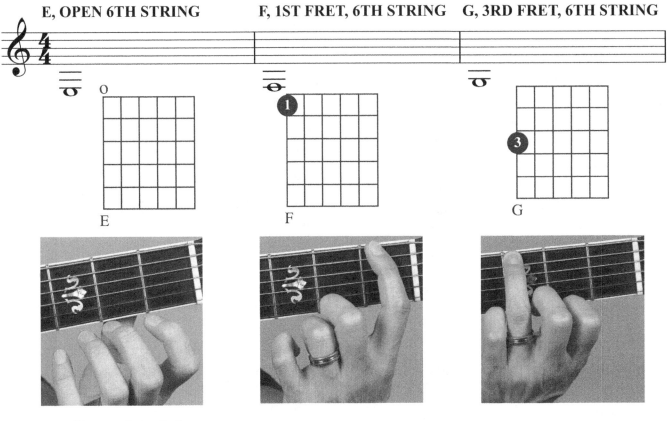

E, OPEN 6TH STRING   **F, 1ST FRET, 6TH STRING**   **G, 3RD FRET, 6TH STRING**

Exercise 36

Practice this exercise playing whole notes.

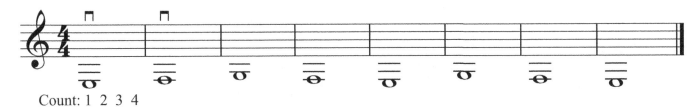

Count: 1 2 3 4

Exercise 37

Practice this exercise playing half notes.

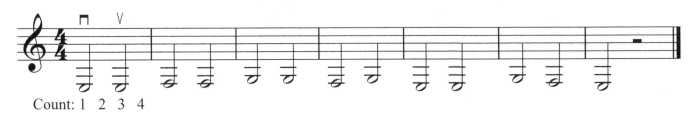

Count: 1   2   3   4

Exercise 38

Practice this exercise primarily playing quarter notes.

Count: 1 2 3 4

Exercise 39

This exercise uses a variety of rhythms. Practice smoothly and evenly.

1ST ENDING, 2ND ENDING

A first ending means to go back to the beginning of the tune or back to a repeat sign and play again. When we return to the first ending a second time, we skip the first ending and play the second ending which now completes the tune.

1st Ending   2nd Ending
1.   2.

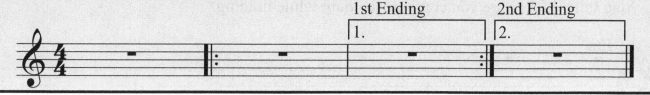

3/4 TIME ARPEGGIOS

This song is in 3/4 time. It uses arpeggios or playing one note of a chord at a time. Practice playing with the band. This time there is a three beat count off.

THE E MINOR PENTATONIC SCALE

This is the E minor pentatonic scale. This scale is one of the most widely used scales on guitar. Practice it slowly at first and then work on speeding up.

HOLD FOR TWO

This song uses the E minor pentatonic scale. It also highlights notes held for a long time. Make sure you continue to count while holding.

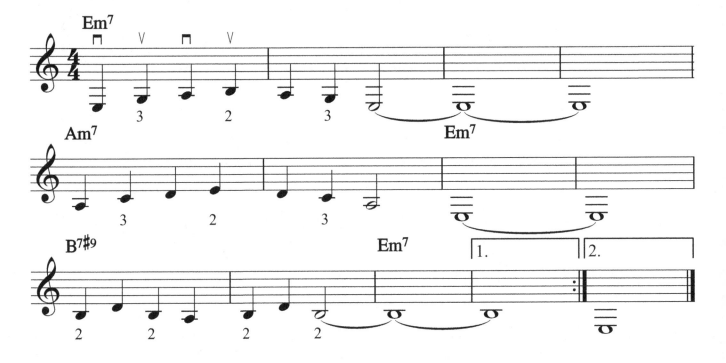

 **TIP**
There are only 12 notes to play but there are an infinite amount of rhythms and dynamics.

SECTION 4
SHARPS, FLATS, AND KEY SIGNATURES

For Online Access to all of the audio files for this course, go to this web address:

http://cvls.com/extras/method/

THE SHARP

A sharp raises a note one fret. One fret higher or lower may also be called a half step. In the example below, we would play F sharp at the 2nd fret 1st string instead of F at the 1st fret 1st string. F sharp is said to be one half step higher than F (or one fret higher). Both sharps and flats are valid for one full measure.

This note is F sharp. It is played one fret higher than F (at the 2nd fret 1st string).

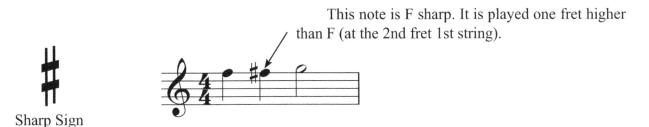

Sharp Sign

THE FLAT

A flat lowers a note one fret. One fret may also be called a half step. In the example below, we would play D flat at the 2nd fret 2nd string instead of D at the 3rd fret 2nd string. D flat is said to be one half step lower than D (or one fret lower)

This note is D flat. It is played one fret lower than D (at the second fret second string).

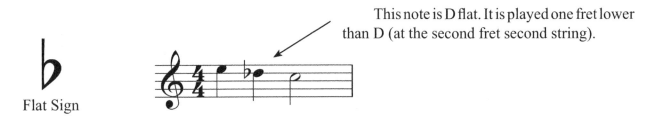

Flat Sign

THE NATURAL

A natural sign means the note is no longer flatted or sharped, but played at its normal position. In the example below, the F sharp is no longer sharped when we see the natural sign and is played back at the 1st fret 1st string. Natural signs are necessary because sharp or flat signs are valid for one full measure. In other words, when a sharp or flat sign is presented in a measure, that note remains sharped or flatted for the rest of the measure unless otherwise indicated.

This note is F natural. It is played at its usual place.

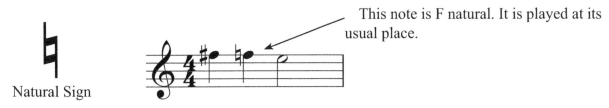

Natural Sign

Exercise 40

Practice this exercise observing the sharps. Follow the fingerings and they will help you play it smoothly and efficiently. Remember a sharp raises a note one half step or one fret higher.

Exercise 41

This exercise has sharps, flats, and naturals. Remember, once a note is sharped or flatted, it remains sharped or flatted throughout the measure unless a natural sign is introduced. A note is no longer sharped or flatted in the next measure unless it has another sharp or flat.

THE CHROMATIC SCALE

Chromatic means moving by half steps or one fret at a time. This chromatic scale is every note in the first position, one after the other. Play this scale slowly and evenly, paying close attention to the fingerings. This is a great exercise for using the 4th finger of the left hand.

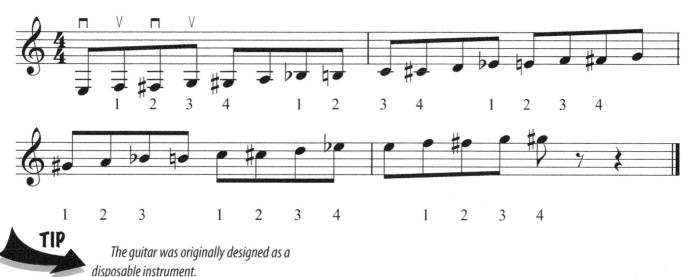

TIP *The guitar was originally designed as a disposable instrument.*

Exercise 42

This exercise will further your acquaintance with sharps and flats.

ACCIDENTAL BOOGIE

This song incorporates accidentals, which is another word for sharps and flats. Practice reading the chromatic tones and pay close attention to the fingerings as they will help you play smooth and efficient. When able, try playing with the band. Wait for a four beat count off to begin.

TIP *Scales are like the alphabet. What you do with them is what creates expression.*

DOTTED NOTES

A dotted note takes the note value (rhythm), and adds half of its value to it. In Example 1 we have a dotted half note. A half note lasts two beats. When it's dotted, we add half of its value to it (2+1=3) and the note now lasts three beats. In Example 2 we have a dotted quarter note. A quarter note usually lasts one beat. Add half of its value to it and it now lasts one and one half beats.

Exercise 43

This exercise highlights the use of dotted rhythms. Count carefully and pay attention to the ties. To help your counting, the beat that each note falls on is included above the staff. If you are unsure of the rhythms, listen to the audio example.

Exercise 44

This time watch the dotted quarter notes. Remember they last one and one half beats. To help you count, the beat that each note falls on is included above the staff. If you are unsure of the rhythms listen to the audio example.

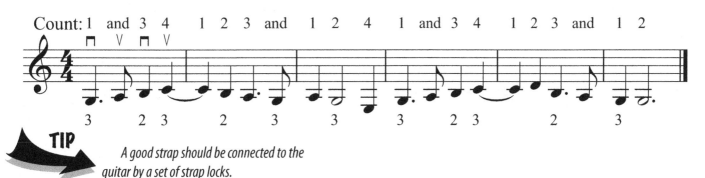

TIP
A good strap should be connected to the guitar by a set of strap locks.

MAJORLY BLUE

Majorly Blue is a blues tune that incorporates accidentals, making it sound brighter. When playing with the band, wait for a four beat count off to start.

CATALONIAN SONG

This famous folk song melody is in 3/4 time. Count 1 and 2 and 3 and, making sure to observe the dotted rhythms. When able, try playing with the track. Wait for the three beat count off to begin.

KEY SIGNATURES

A key signature tells us what notes are flatted or sharped throughout the tune. It's name also tells us what key we are in. In Example 1, the sharp is located on the top line where the note F would normally be played. This means that throughout this tune the note F, wherever it is found, (not just on the top line of the staff) is sharped unless otherwise indicated. This also tells us the song is in the key of G. The key of G has one sharp, F sharp, and this can be seen when playing a G major scale in Example 2.

Key Signature

EXAMPLE 1

The note F is sharped.

EXAMPLE 2: THE G MAJOR SCALE

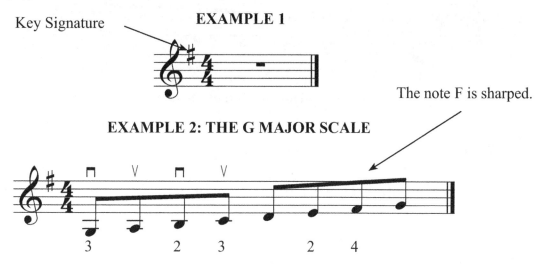

This is in contrast to C major which has no sharps or flats in it. Look at Example 3 and 4.

Key Signature
(no sharps or flats)

EXAMPLE 3

EXAMPLE 4: THE C MAJOR SCALE

TIP

Never use furniture polish on your guitar.
Use guitar polish and a guitar cloth.

45

In Example 5, we have one flat in the key signature. This is located on the third line of the staff where the note B would normally be played. Because of this key signature, the note B will be flatted (one fret lower) throughout this tune or exercise. This is also the key of F which is seen in Example 6.

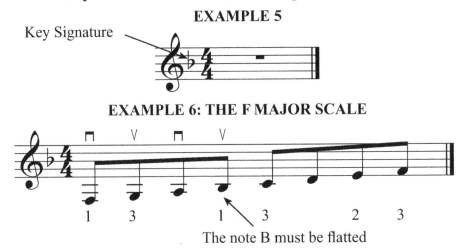

Exercise 45

This exercise highlights the use of the F sharp in the key signature (the key of G major). The note F must be sharped wherever it is found in this exercise.

Exercise 46

There is a B flat in the key signature of this exercise (the key of F major). Every B in this melody must be flatted. The B flat in measure 6 can be found at the 3rd fret 3rd string.

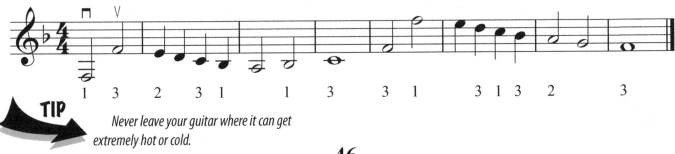

TIP *Never leave your guitar where it can get extremely hot or cold.*

CARELESS LOVE

Careless Love is a well known traditional tune with a great melody. The key signature tells us we are in the key of G. This means every time you find the note F, you must sharp it and play F sharp. Try playing with the band. Wait for the four beat count off to start.

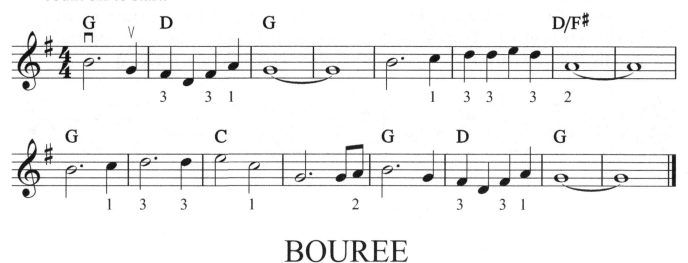

BOUREE

This is a classical melody written by Robert de Visee. Watch the B flat in the key signature and take note of the repeat sign at the end. In the full tune there is more to this melody (we are only playing the first half). When you can play this comfortably, try playing with the track. There will be a three beat count off before you start. It is only three counts because the first measure is a pick up. You must begin to play on beat four.

Note - This piece is a duet for two guitars. There are three tracks - Track 41 is the duet with both guitars, Track 42 is the 2nd guitar along with metronome, and Track 43 is the 2nd guitar by itself so you can practice or use in a student recital.

Solos are a combination of scales, arpeggios, licks, and expression.

MINUET IN G

This is another classical melody and this time by J. S. Bach. This famous melody is presented in the key of G. Take note that it is in 3/4 time. In the full piece there is more to this melody (we are only playing the first half). Wait for the three beat count off to start playing with the accompaniment.

Note - This piece is a duet for two guitars. There are three tracks - Track 44 is the duet with both guitars, Track 45 is the 2nd guitar along with metronome, and Track 46 is the 2nd guitar by itself so you can practice or use in a student recital.

HIGH PEDAL IN G

This tune highlights the use of a high pedal tone on the open third string. Use alternate picking or finding the correct string to play will prove difficult. When playing with the band, wait for the four beat count off to start.

TIP *The **Let's Jam CDs** are great for practicing scales and licks.*

SECTION 5
HARMONY AND CHORDS

For Online Access to all of the audio files for this course, go to this web address:

http://cvls.com/extras/method/

Playing more than one note at a time results in what is called harmony. Playing three or more notes at a time is generally going to be called a chord. Music notation tells us to play more than one note at a time by stacking the notes on top of each other in the same vertical space. Example 1 is an example of harmony. We are to play both the notes C and E at the same time. Example 2 is a series of harmonized notes. Example 3 is an example of a chord. We are to play all three notes: C, E, and G at the same time. This makes a C major chord or what is also called a triad.

Example 4 is a D major chord. Even though we are playing four strings at the same time, we are really only playing three different notes, D on the fourth string, A on the third string, another D on the second string, and the note F sharp on the first string. Take note of the F sharp in the key signature.

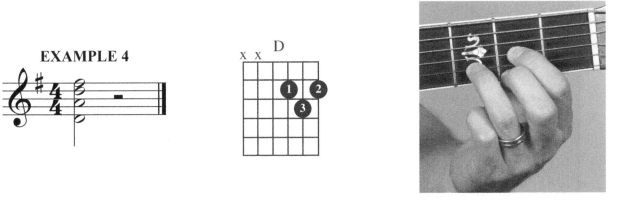

Example 5 is an E minor chord. We are playing all six strings at the same time but once again only three different notes. E on the 6th string, B on the 5th string, E on the 4th string, G on the 3rd string, B on the 2nd string, and E on the 1st string (E, G, B).

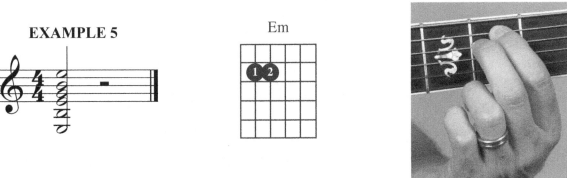

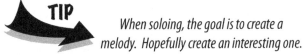

TIP

When soloing, the goal is to create a melody. Hopefully create an interesting one.

50

Exercise 47

This exercise is a two note harmony with a low melody. The lower notes are written as eighth notes but let them ring as you play the higher notes. Play all of this exercise using downstrokes. Notice your first finger never has to leave the 1st fret 2nd string.

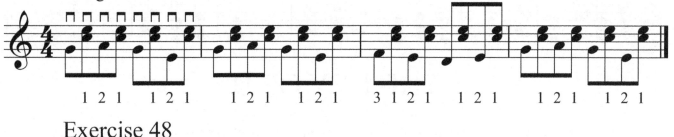

Exercise 48

This exercise has a three note harmony with a lower melody. Once again let all of the notes ring during this exercise. Notice the fingerings for the last chord (Em) are placed next to the notes they are to play. This is a common way to write fingerings when playing several notes at a time.

CHORD PLAY

The chord is first played as an arpeggio and then as a chord to be strummed. The first four notes of the measure create the chord. Leave the left fingers pressing down and let them ring to create the full chord. Notice the fingering below the staff.

Exercise 49

This is a chordal exercise. Use your note reading skills to identify the notes of each chord. The fingerings are presented the first time you see the chord but are omitted the next time. This tells the player to use the same fingerings the next time.

THE KEY OF D

The key of D has two sharps, F sharp and C sharp. When you see this key signature you must sharp every F and C sharp unless told otherwise.

Key Signature   **KEY OF D**

Exercise 50

This exercise is the D major scale. Remember to sharp any C or F you play.

D MELODY

This tune is in the key of D. Let the notes ring whenever possible. Wait for the four beat count off when playing with the track.

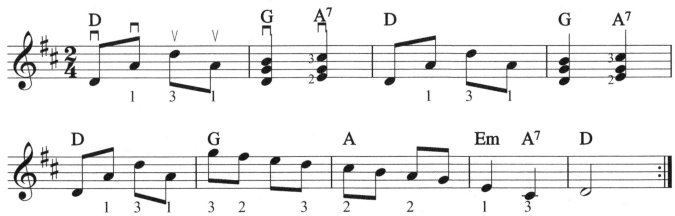

ARPEGGIATION

Here is another song in the key of D. These are arpeggios so let all the notes ring whenever possible. The trick to playing this type of tune is to visualize and make the whole chord at the start of each arpeggio. To help you get accustomed to this idea, the chord diagrams for each arpeggio are provided. As you progress, you will begin to identify these chords on your own. Pay close attention to the fingering and notice the descending D major scale in bar 8. When you are comfortable playing this tune try playing with the band. Wait for the four beat count off to begin.

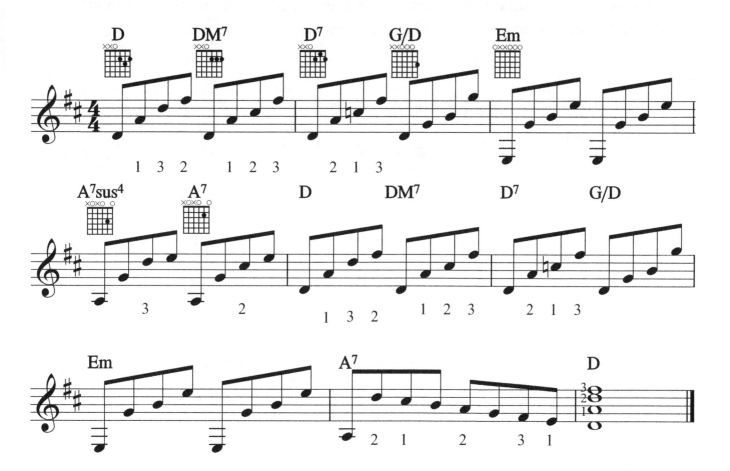

When playing guitar, use the lightest touch possible with the left hand so that youl get a clear note.

53

WAYFARING STRANGER

This well known melody is in E minor. E minor has the same key signature as G major. This is referred to as relative major and minor. G major and E minor are said to be relative because they both have only one sharp in the key signature (F sharp). Watch the ties and chord shapes while working on this tune. Take special note of the lower notes that are whole notes and ring while upper notes are played. The first time we see this is in the third measure. Keep these notes ringing and leave the fingers in place while you play the upper notes. When you are comfortable playing this tune, try playing with the band. There is a pick up at the beginning so you will come in on the second half of beat three. Count 1 and 2 and 3, coming in on the next "and" of the beat. This tune also works well as a solo piece.

TIP

A good teacher can dramatically increase your rate of learning.

54

G BLUES

This blues in G highlights some great blues lines. Watch out for the accidentals and the challenging rhythms. When you are able, try playing with the band. Wait for the four beat count off to start.

PLAYING B IN TWO PLACES

We have been playing the note B on the middle line of the staff on the open 2nd string. We can also play this note on the 3rd string 4th fret. They are exactly the same note played on different strings. As you progress with your note reading and move up the guitar neck, you will find there are several places to play the same notes on the guitar. In order to play the next song, we will need to play the note B on the open 2nd string and at the 4th fret 3rd string.

THE NOTE B

This note may be played on the open second string or the 4th fret 3rd string. Play this note in both places and compare. They are the same.

Have your guitar set up twice a year. Once in the spring and once in the fall.

KEMP'S JIG

Here is another famous folk melody. It is meant to be played as a solo piece so there is no accompanying track. This is a challenging tune to read so be patient and practice slowly. Notice the fingerings and the notes that are ringing while others are being played. Take special note of the first and second endings. The first ending repeat sign takes you back to the previous repeat sign (bar 9), not the beginning of the tune.

*For more scales try **The Guitarist's Scale Book** by Watch & Learn.*

THE KEY OF E

The key signature for the key of E has four sharps, F sharp, C sharp, G sharp, and D sharp. Every F, C, G and D are to be sharped in this key unless told otherwise. At first this may be hard to keep track of, but with practice you will get used to this key. The key of E is an extremely common key for guitar so you must become comfortable reading and playing in this key.

Exercise 51

This exercise is the E major scale. Practice it until you can play it smoothly. Pay attention to the fingering, especially when you get to the note B in the middle of the staff. This note is to be played on the 3rd string 4th fret.

CASCADE IN E

This melody in E sounds best if you let the notes ring together in a cascading like sound. Keep an eye on the fingerings and take special note of the B in measure five which is played at the 4th fret 3rd string. When you are comfortable playing this tune, try playing with the band. Wait for the four beat count off to begin.

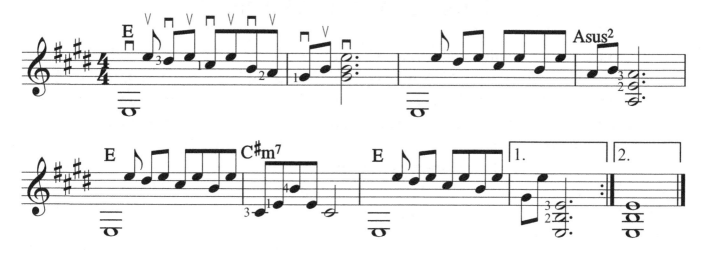

TIP *The Guitarist's Chord Book* has virtually every chord you will ever need.

E BLUES DOUBLE STOPS

Double stop means to play two notes at once. It is another way to say harmony.
Watch the accidentals and the rest bars. Once you are able, try playing with the band.
Wait for the four beat count off to start.

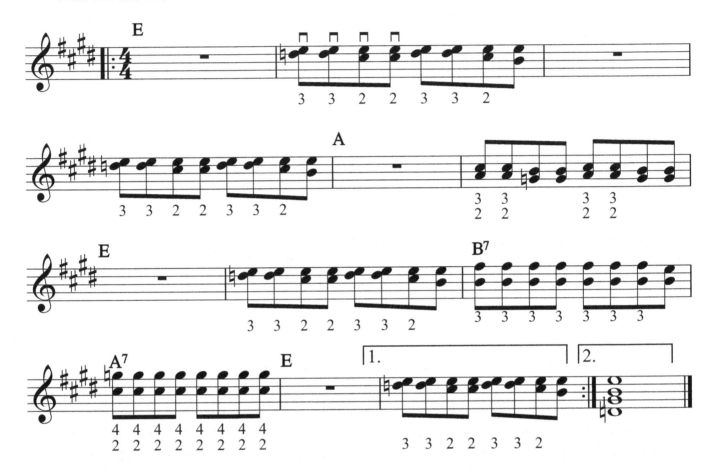

CONGRATULATIONS!

You have now completed *Guitar Method 1* by *Watch & Learn*. The follow-up to
this course is *Guitar Method 2*. You may want to try our other guitar products like *The
Guitarist's Scale Book* or *The Guitarist's Chord Book*. If you are looking to increase
your music theory knowledge, try *The Guitarist's Music Theory Book*. Courses like
Introduction to Blues Guitar or *Introduction to Rock Guitar* would be a great way to
increase your guitar playing abilities as well.

Wherever you go from here, we hope you have increased your knowledge and
enjoyment of the guitar. Once again, congratulations on finishing this course.

 *To change strings, you should have a set of
wire cutters and a peg winder.*

Made in the USA
Monee, IL
06 November 2020

46873482R00037